WELCOME

Dear _____,

I look forward to being your teacher this year. Together with your new friends, we will have fun learning and celebrating many things. You are very special and God loves you very much.

       Love,

_____

God Bless You!

Come and discover God's love!

I AM SPECIAL.

From: _____

_____

_____

To: _____

_____

_____

_____

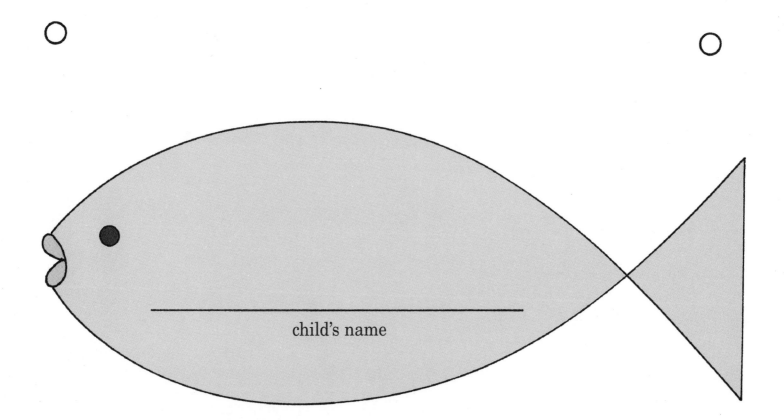

child's name

 I AM SPECIAL®

See what I can do!

I can hang up my coat.

I can pray.

I can sing.

I can put away my toys.

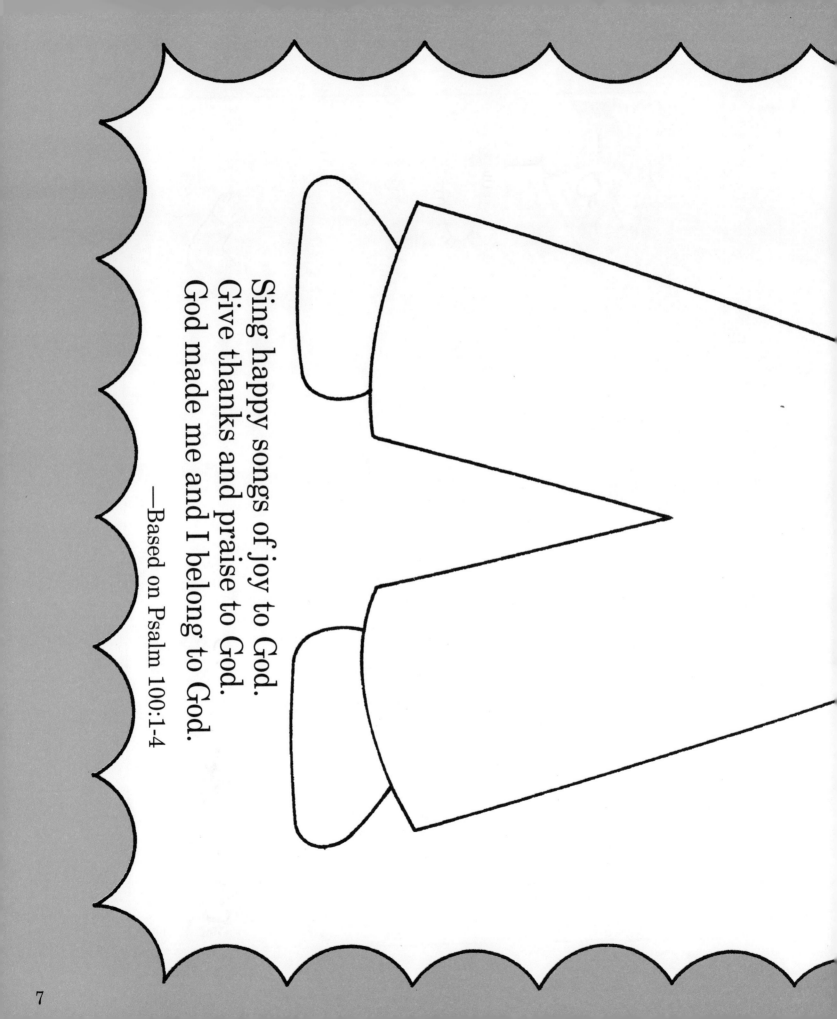

Sing happy songs of joy to God.
Give thanks and praise to God.
God made me and I belong to God.

—Based on Psalm 100:1-4

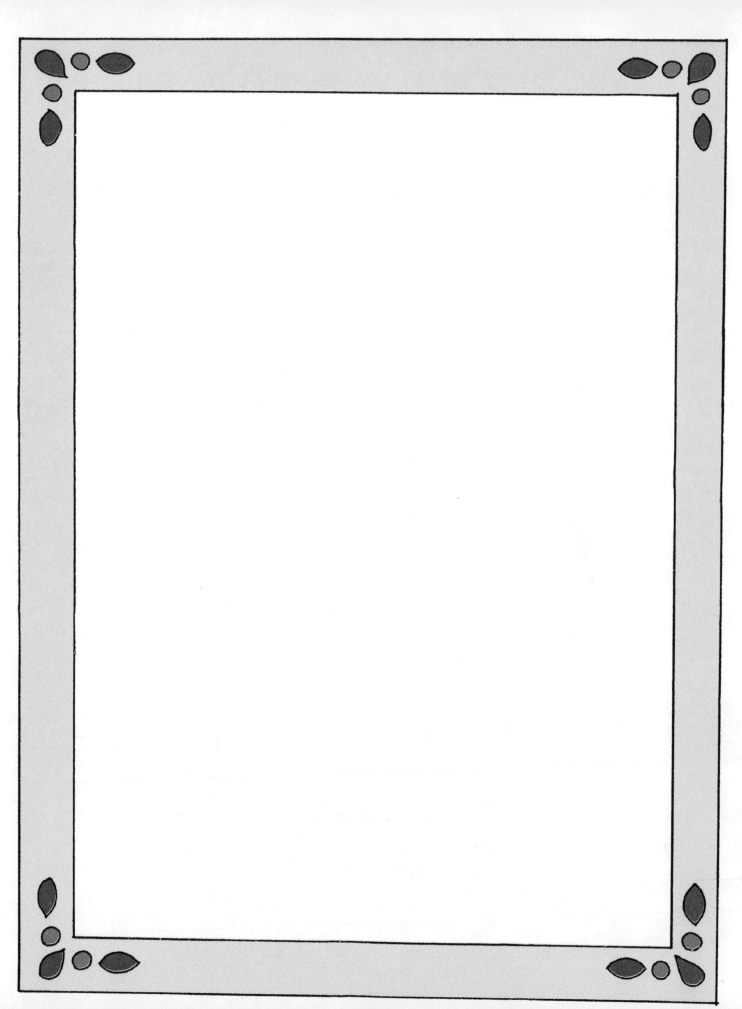

I can _____.

Family Tree

Family Tree

Family Tree

Family Tree

12

Let's be friends!

"Love one another."

John 15:12

Happy
Friends
Day!

I Am Special!

You Are Special!

Dear _____ ,

Date _____

God loves you and made you special.

Here is a picture I made for you.

From your friend,

_____

Two Families

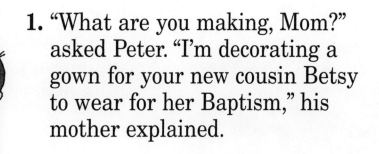

1. "What are you making, Mom?" asked Peter. "I'm decorating a gown for your new cousin Betsy to wear for her Baptism," his mother explained.

2. "What does Baptism mean?" asked Peter. "Baptism is a special celebration at church when a person is welcomed into God's family," his mother said. "Betsy will belong to her own small family and also to God's very big family."

3. "Was I ever baptized?" asked Peter. "Yes, there you are in your white gown," replied Mother. "Our pastor poured water on your forehead.... We need water for living, drinking, washing, cooking, and swimming."

4. "This is the candle that was lit at your Baptism," his mother explained. "When we see a candle, we feel happy and think of Jesus."

5. At Betsy's Baptism, Peter watched as water was carefully poured on her forehead and her own candle was lit. "Now Betsy has two families, just like me!" thought Peter.

6. What a happy celebration!

GOD BLESS BETSY

Based on "Two Families," ©1986 by Carol Therese Plum.
Modified by permission.

We Need Water

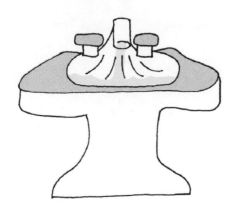

Thank you, God, for water.

We Celebrate Baptism

"_____(Name)_____, I baptize you in the name of the Father, and of the Son, and of the Holy Spirit."

God made
the sun.

God made
the moon
and stars.

God's
wonderful
world.

Thank
you,
God!

19

God made
the flowers.

God made
the trees.

God's
wonderful
world.

Thank
you,
God!

God made
the birds.

God made
the animals.

God's
wonderful
world.

Thank
you,
God!

God made
me.

God made
fish.

God's
wonderful
world.

Thank
you,
God!

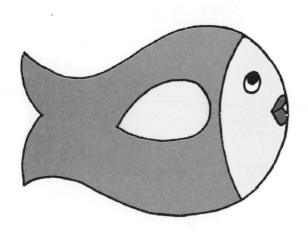

25

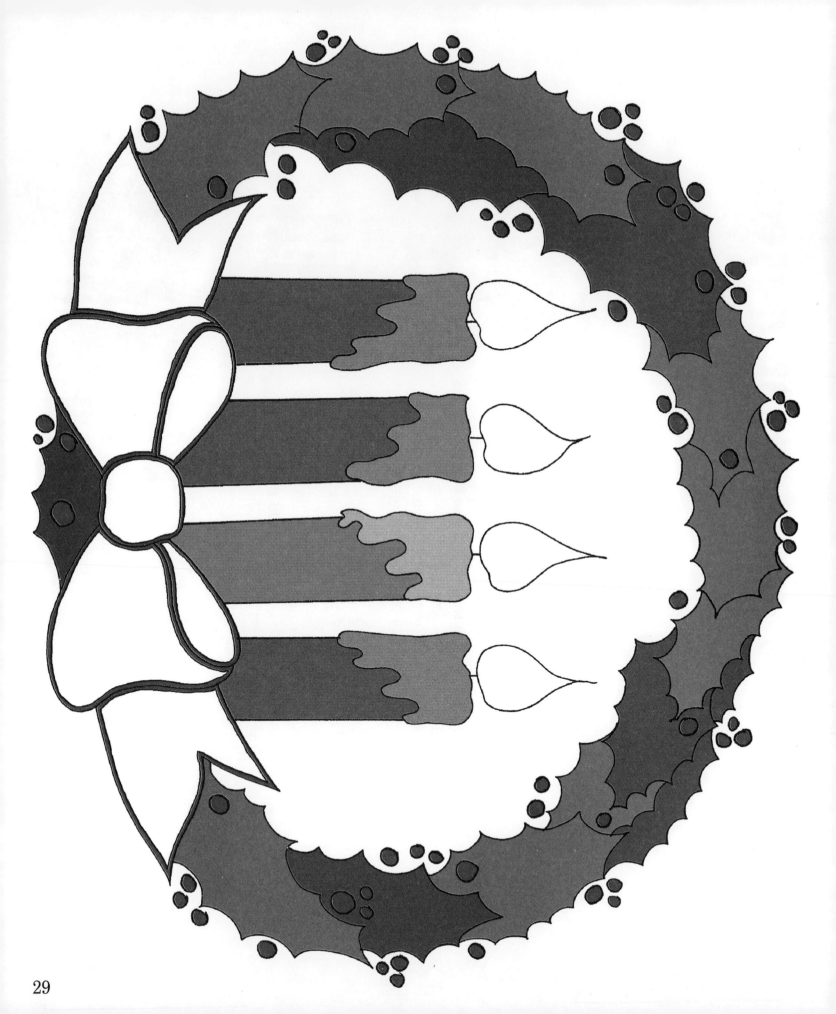

29

Family Advent Prayers

Each Sunday of Advent the family gathers around the Advent wreath and lights an additional candle. The following prayers can be used:

First Sunday: (light one candle)
Dear God, bless this wreath and help our family to remember that Christmas is a time to celebrate Jesus' birthday.

Second Sunday: (light two candles)
Dear God, as we decorate our home for Christmas, we think about the birth of your only Son, Jesus. Help us to show love and kindness toward each other as we get ready to celebrate his birthday.

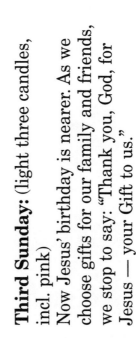

Third Sunday: (light three candles, incl. pink)
Now Jesus' birthday is nearer. As we choose gifts for our family and friends, we stop to say: "Thank you, God, for Jesus — your Gift to us."

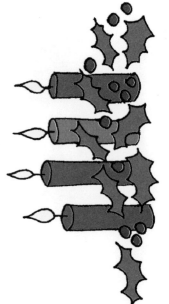

Fourth Sunday: (light four candles)
Now Jesus' birthday is very near. May his birthday bring joy and happiness to all of us as we try to be more like Jesus every day.

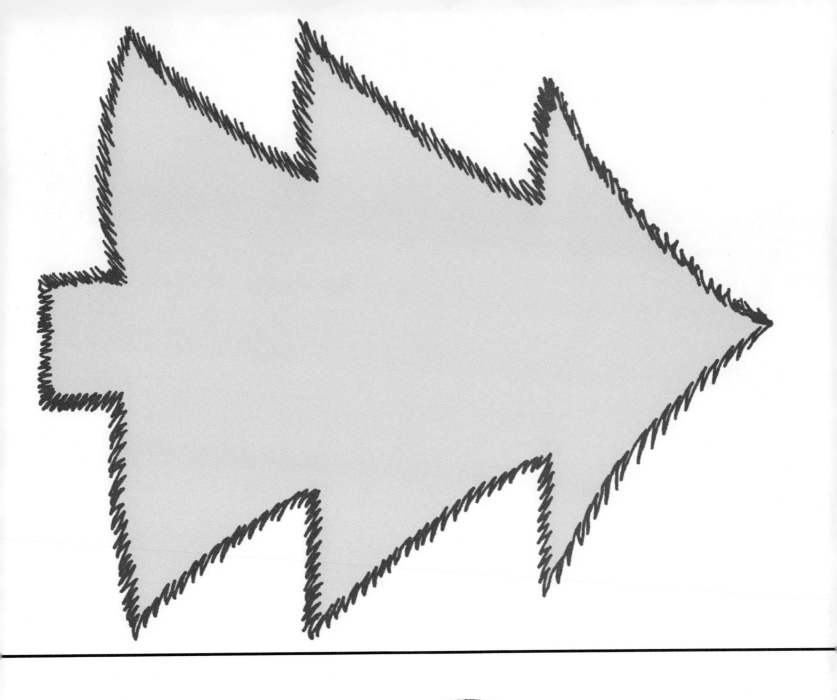

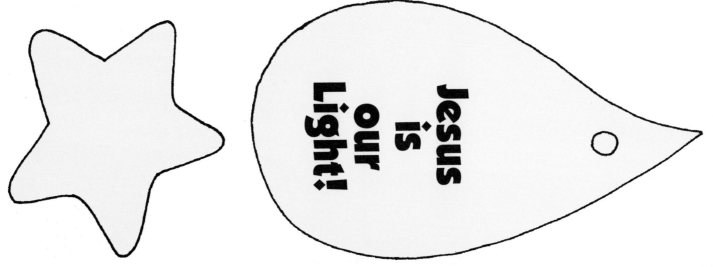

Jesus
is
our
Light!

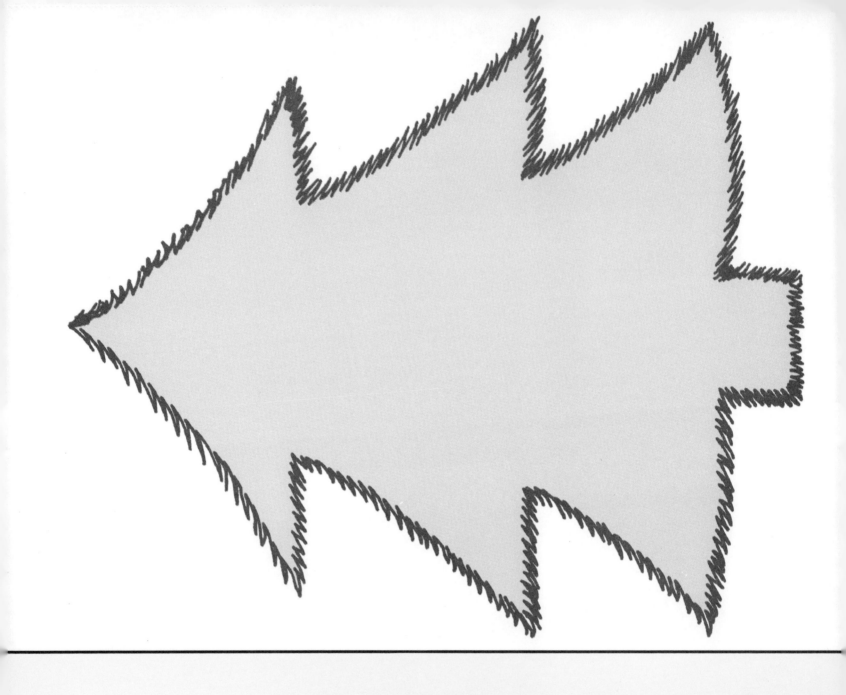

(childs name)

leg   leg   manger bed (cut on solid lines/fold on dotted lines)

Bell

A reminder that Jesus' birthday is coming. Ringing bells at Christmas is a joyful way to celebrate his birthday.

Candle

A candle reminds us that Jesus and his words are like a light that guides us. We think of Jesus and feel happy when we see a candle light glowing.

Star

A bright star shone in the sky and guided the Wise Men to find baby Jesus.

Gift

God gave his Son, Jesus, as a gift to help us. The Wise Men brought gifts to baby Jesus soon after he was born. We give presents to our family and friends at Christmas because we love them and want them to feel happy.

Peter Can't Wait

1. Peter and his family listened to hear the ringmaster loudly announce, "Let the circus begin!"

2. Peter jumped in his seat when three elephants paraded to the loud marching music of trumpets and drums.

3. Next, the orchestra played a soft, quiet melody as trapeze artists swung gracefully, high up in the air.

4. Peter gave a shriek when the lion in a circus wagon roared ferociously.

5. The audience laughed and laughed as funny clowns chased one another with buckets of water and cream pies.

6. Much to Peter's surprise, he was chosen to ride in the clowns' fire engine and ring the clanging bell. "Wow!" Peter explained. "I really did get to join the circus."

Based on "Peter Can't Wait," ©1991 by Carol Therese Plum. Modified by permission.

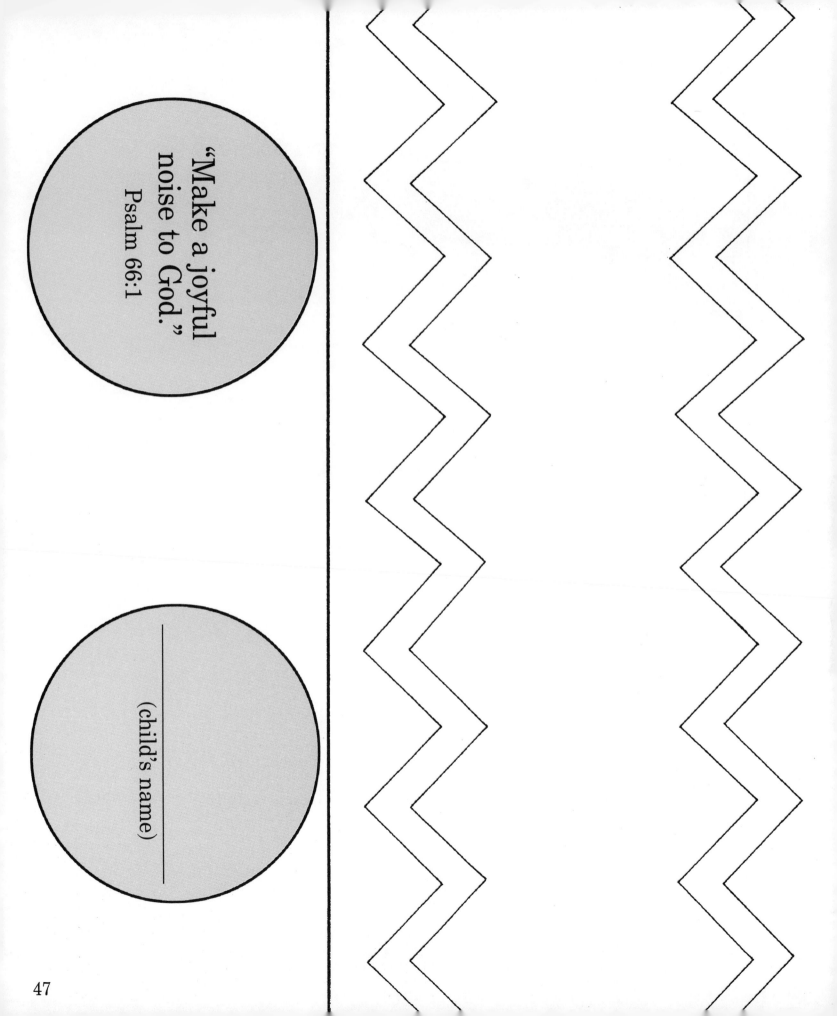

"Make a joyful
noise to God."
Psalm 66:1

_____
(child's name)

47

God said, "See, I give you . . . every tree that has seed-bearing fruit on it to be your food."

Genesis 1:29

49

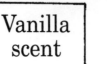

Vanilla
scent

My Favorite Things to Smell

Mint
scent

Thank you, God, for the sense of smell!

Coconut
scent

50

Things I like to see.			
Things I like to touch.			
Things I like to hear.			
Things I like to smell.			SOAP
Things I like to taste.			

51

Matching Tastes . . .

sweet

spicy

salty

sour

Thank you, God, for the sense of taste.

Jesus "went about doing good."
Acts 10:38

4. Jesus asks children to be kind and to help others as he did.

1. Jesus helped people who were sick.

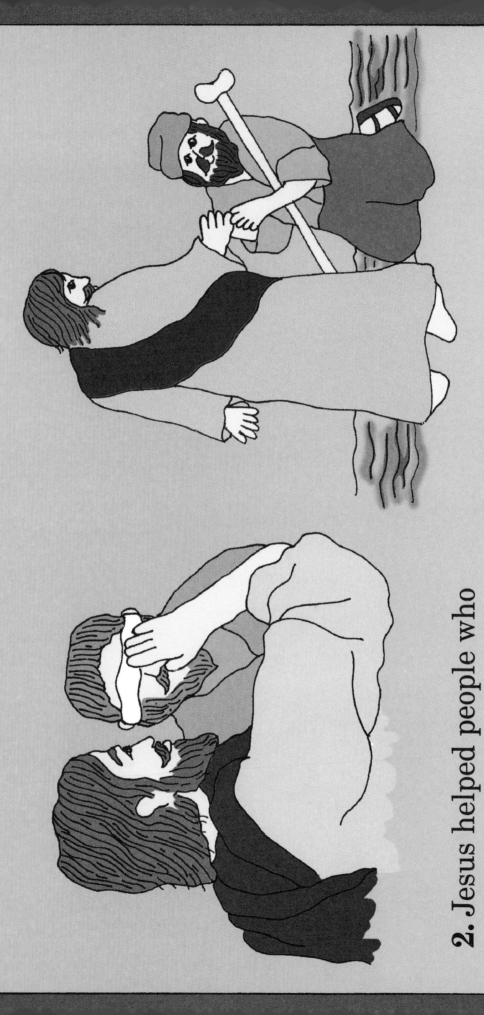

3. Jesus helped people who could not walk.

2. Jesus helped people who could not see.

I can help

◆

Friends of Jesus help one another.

From Galatians 6:10

_____

has climbed the
Mountain of Love!

♥ I said a prayer.
_____

♥ I set the table.
_____

♥ I made my bed.
_____

♥ I helped clean up after supper.
_____

♥ I put away toys.
_____

♥ I smiled at my teacher.
_____

♥ I drew a picture for a friend.
_____

♥ I remembered to say "please"
    and "thank you."
_____

♥ I invited a friend to play.
_____

♥ I took turns during play time.
_____

Mountain of Love

62

One to keep — One to share.

63

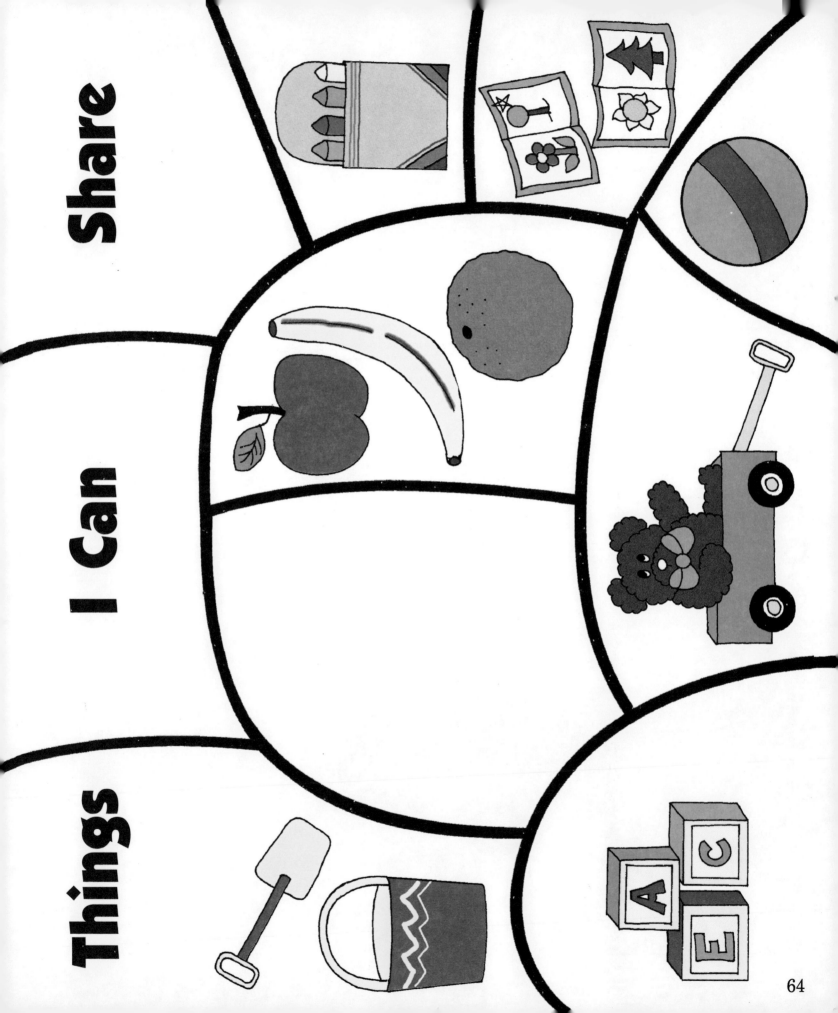

Share

I Can

Things

64

Leaf and Flower Buds

From the Holy Bible we learn that in the beginning God said, "Let the earth bring forth every kind of plant that bears seed and every kind of fruit tree that bears fruit with its seed in it." And so it happened. And God saw that it was good.

From Genesis 1:11-12

Thank you, God, for my favorite fruit!

Leaf Buds in Spring

1. See the bud.

2. See the bud opening.

3. See the leaf.

Thank you, God, for new life in spring!

Flower Buds in Spring

1. See the bud.

2. See the bud opening.

3. See the flower.

Jesus is alive.
Alleluia! Alleluia!

4. However, on the third day after Jesus died, the most wonderful thing happened! His friends discovered that Jesus had not left them. Jesus was alive again, and he returned to his friends. Jesus had kept his promise. Easter is a happy day! Easter is a day to celebrate!

The Easter Story
(Holy Week)

1. Jesus traveled throughout the country helping people and telling them about God's love for them. One day when Jesus rode into Jerusalem on a donkey, his friends were so happy to see him that they cheered and waved palm branches.

77

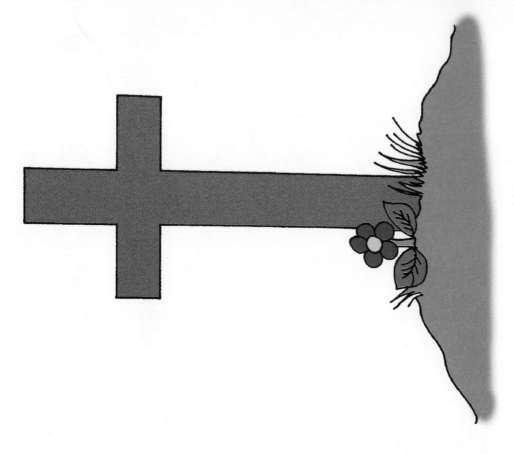

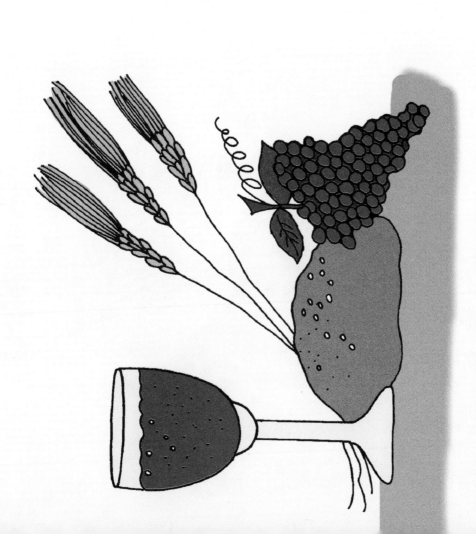

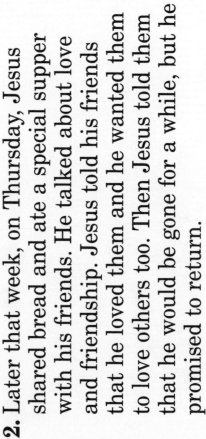

3. Some people were not his friends. They did not like what he was teaching about God. The next day, they arranged to have him die on a cross. His friends felt very sad. They thought that he would be gone forever.

2. Later that week, on Thursday, Jesus shared bread and ate a special supper with his friends. He talked about love and friendship. Jesus told his friends that he loved them and he wanted them to love others too. Then Jesus told them that he would be gone for a while, but he promised to return.

Jesus is our Light!

Happy Easter!

The Happy-Sad Birthday Party

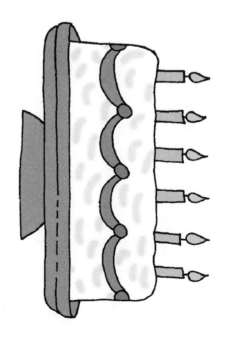

©1991 by Carol Therese Plum. Modified by permission.

8. After his nap, Amy surprised Peter with a balloon and piece of cake. "I'm glad you came, Amy," said Peter. "I don't feel sad any more."

6. Peter started to cry. "I don't want to stay home! All my friends will be there."

3. Peter helped his mother wrap a present for Amy. Then he went out to play.

7. "Hi, Peter," said Carolyn. "I thought you would like to hear some stories. Maybe they'll make you feel better."

5. "Peter," said his father. "I'm afraid you won't be able to go to Amy's birthday party tomorrow."

2. "Hooray!" Peter explained. "Amy is going to have a birthday party, and all our friends will be there. We'll have so much fun!"

4. When his father called him for dinner, Peter slipped and fell from the tree he had climbed.

84

Peter's Angry Toy's

1. "Peter," said his father, "I want you to pick up these toys."
"No!" snapped Peter, shaking his head. "I don't want to."
"Well," his father replied, "then go to your room until you
decide to do what you've been told."

2. With anger, Peter stomped up the stairs
to his room and hopped into bed. It
wasn't fair that he should have to put
away the toys when his friend Tony had
played with them too. "I'm not going to
do it," Peter thought, closing his eyes.

3. In a dream, Peter decided to pick up his toys, but they wouldn't stay in the box. They marched, jumped, hopped, somersaulted right back out saying, "We won't be picked up; we won't be put away!" "Why won't you listen to me?" Peter shouted.

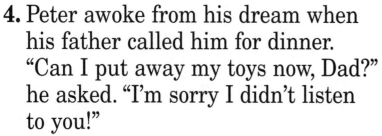

4. Peter awoke from his dream when his father called him for dinner. "Can I put away my toys now, Dad?" he asked. "I'm sorry I didn't listen to you!"

"I forgive you, Peter," said his father, "and I'm glad you feel better now."

5. Peter wasn't angry anymore. He gave his dad a big hug and put away his toys.

Based on "Peter's Angry Toys" ©1991 by Carol Therese Plum. Modified by permission.

86

This is something I fear.

This is someone I can talk to.

87

Feelings Wheel

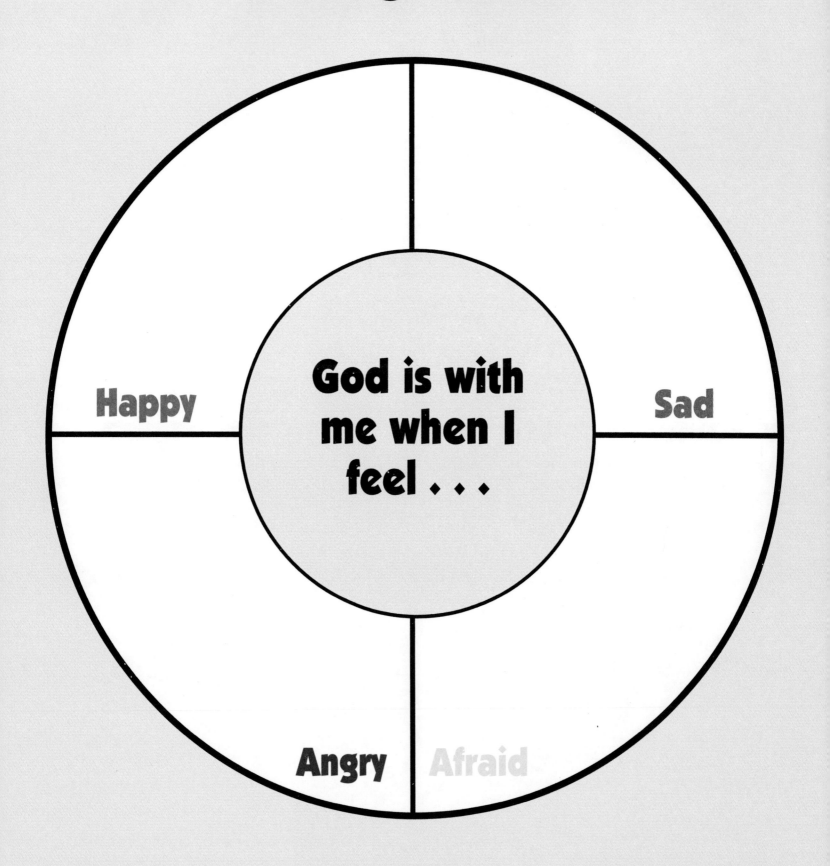

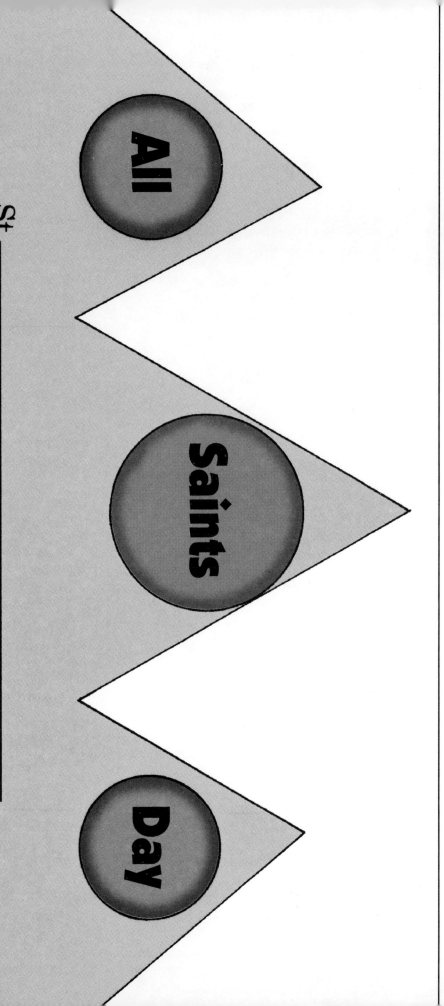

All

Saints

Day

St. _____

Saint of the future!

A

B

A

B

(head band)

(extra head band)

A

B

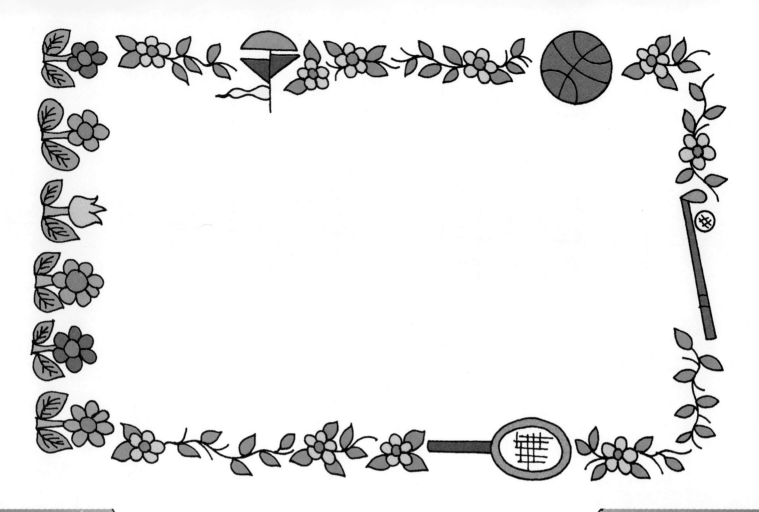

God loves you!

Have a happy day!

Dear _____,

You are special

to me because _____

_____

_____

Love, _____

I ♥ YOU!

Have a happy day!

God loves you!

Dear _____,

You are special

to me because _____

_____

_____

Love, _____

I 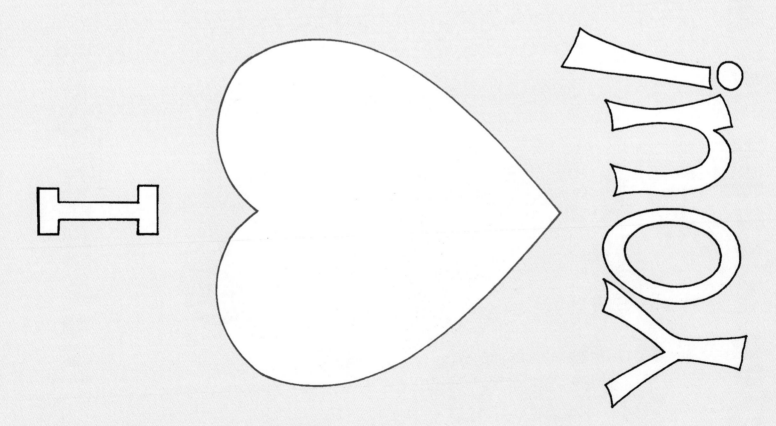 YOU!

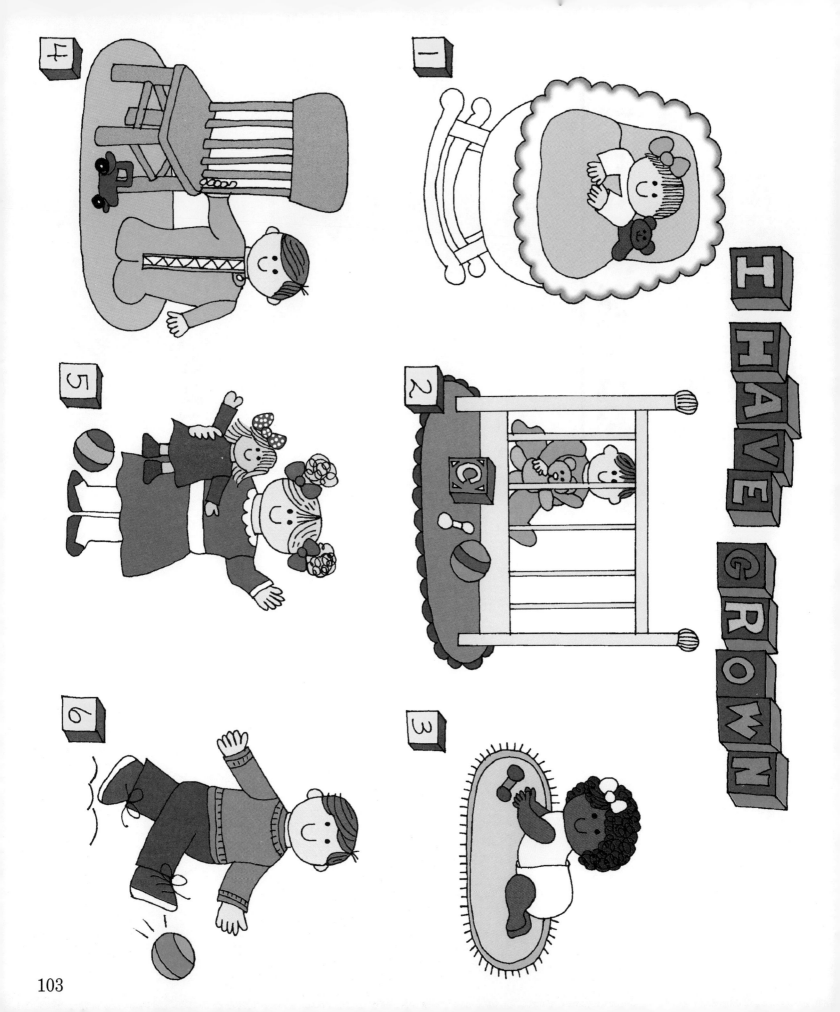

I HAVE GROWN

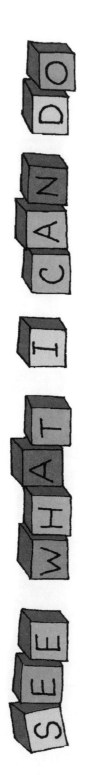

SEE WHAT I CAN DO

THANK YOU GOD!

"Love one another."

From: _____
_____
_____

Stamp

You are special!

God loves you!

You Are Invited!

To: _____
_____
_____
_____

You are invited to our End-of-the-Year Celebration to praise and thank God for a happy year with our teachers, families, and friends.

Date: _____

Time: _____

Place: _____

I Am Special!

I am growing.

Thank you, God,
for loving me.
Help me to
love others too!
Amen.

This is to certify that

_____

has completed the
I Am Special® Program.

As you grow, may
you continue to be the
special person
God wants you to be.

_____
teacher/catechist

_____   _____
date   school/parish

I am a child of God!

(photo of my baptismal day)

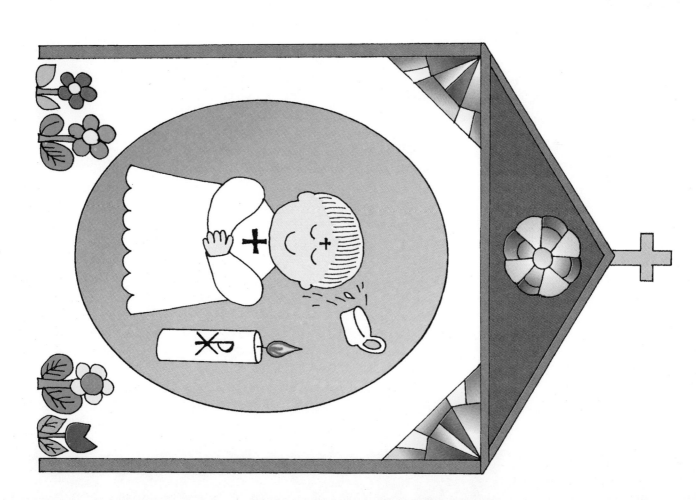

Happy Baptismal Day!

Congratulations

and

God Bless You

Always

(teacher/catechist)

I

_____
(name)

was baptized into

God's family on

_____
(date)

Church: _____

Priest/Deacon: _____

Godparents: _____

112